A DAY THAT MADE HISTORY

D-DAY

Anne Grimshaw

Dryad Press Limited   London

Contents

Acknowledgments

I would like to thank the following people for all their help and encouragement in the writing of this book: D-Day veteran Sid Kemp; Bernard Williams and Rod Jones for advising and proof-reading; Lt. Col. Mike Martin and Mick Irwin who accompanied my tour of the Normandy beaches; and Harold Howard of Lynchburg, Virginia, who first prompted me to go to Normandy. The author and publishers wish to thank the following for their kind permission to reproduce copyright illustrations: BBC Hulton Picture Library, pages 12, 32, 39 (top), 60; Imperial War Museum, pages 4, 5, 15, 29, 36, 38, 39 (bottom), 40, 41, 46, 54, 55; The Photo Source, pages 10, 13, 34, 59, 62; Portsmouth Publishing and Printing Ltd, pages 7, 14, 50; Ullstein Bilderdienst, pages 9, 22, 51. The pictures were researched by David Pratt.

The "Day that Made History" series was devised by Nathaniel Harris.

To Mum and Dad

© Anne Grimshaw 1988. First published 1988.

Typeset by Tek-Art Ltd, Kent, and printed and bound by Richard Clay Ltd, Chichester, Sussex for the publishers, Dryad Press Limited, 8 Cavendish Square, London W1M 0AJ

British Library Cataloguing in Publication Data

Grimshaw, Anne
  D-Day : the Normandy landings. — (A Day
  that made history).
  1. World War 2. Normandy campaign. D-Day.
  1944- For schools
  I. Title   II. Series
  940.54'21

ISBN 0-85219-763-2

THE EVENTS

Bénouville, 0016 hours, 6 June 1944

The glider's wings tore through the reeds. In the marshy ground alongside the Caen Canal the silent craft lurched to a standstill, its nose caught in the barbed wire entanglement. On board, shaken by the crash landing but ready for action, was a small group of men of the 6th Airborne Division.

Their leader, Major John Howard, glanced at his watch. It was 0016 hours on 6 June 1944. His platoon, consisting of about thirty men of the 2nd Battalion Oxfordshire and Buckinghamshire Light Infantry and some Royal Engineers (sappers), scrambled out of the glider. Their objective was the bridge which carried the road over the canal to the village of Bénouville. Its curved silhouette stood out against the night sky just 50 metres away.

In the darkness the water to the men's left glittered in the fitful moonlight. On the far bank of the canal was the dark shape of the Gondrées' café. Now two more gliders slewed to a halt behind the first. They too disgorged their platoons. The men, their faces blackened, ran silently towards the German pillbox which guarded the entrance to the bridge.

A German sentry, Helmut Romer, was pacing his beat nervously. Most of his officers were at a birthday party in Caen, 16 kilometres inland, but he could hear some of his comrades talking in the pillbox. Otherwise, all was quiet. He had heard a muffled crash a few moments before, but took it to be a distant enemy bomber shot down by anti-aircraft guns. Suddenly there was shooting all around, smoke from phosphorous smoke bombs, the explosion of hand grenades lobbed into the pillbox, a burst of machine-gun fire, screaming and cursing and the ricocheting of bullets off the steel bridge. There was a splash as someone fell into the water, a groan and a dull thud as a man was shot. Helmut Romer dived in to a nearby trench for cover, unable to alert the rest of the guard.

21 ARMY GROUP

PERSONAL MESSAGE
FROM THE C-in-C

To be read out to all Troops

1. The time has come to deal the enemy a terrific blow in Western Europe.

The blow will be struck by the combined sea, land, and air forces of the Allies—together constituting one great Allied team, under the supreme command of General Eisenhower.

2. On the eve of this great adventure I send my best wishes to every soldier in the Allied team.

To us is given the honour of striking a blow for freedom which will live in history; and in the better days that lie ahead men will speak with pride of our doings. We have a great and a righteous cause.

Let us pray that "The Lord Mighty in Battle" will go forth with our armies, and that His special providence will aid us in the struggle.

3. I want every soldier to know that I have complete confidence in the successful outcome of the operations that we are now about to begin.

With stout hearts, and with enthusiasm for the contest, let us go forward to victory.

4. And, as we enter the battle, let us recall the words of a famous soldier spoken many years ago:—

> "He either fears his fate too much,
>   Or his deserts are small,
> Who dare not put it to the touch,
>   To win or lose it all."

5. Good luck to each one of you. And good hunting on the mainland of Europe.

B. L. Montgomery
General
C.-in-C 21 Army Group.

1944.

Personal message to all troops from General Montgomery.

The leading section from the first glider ran over the bridge. They were all firing from the hip. Their leader, Lt Don Brotheridge, fell wounded. (He was dragged to safety but died later.) Surprised and unnerved by the attack, the Germans fled, leaving their weapons behind.

Across the canal, awakened by the din, Monsieur and Madame Gondrée leaned out of the upstairs windows of their café.

After ten minutes, the British had control of the bridge. Patrols had been sent out to secure landing zones for the

Crashed gliders alongside the Caen Canal. The Gondrées' cafe can be seen in the background between the trees, and the bridge is just visible above the right-hand glider.

paratroopers. When they arrived, these men would form the left flank of an invading force which was to assault the French coast from east of Caen to the Cotentin Peninsula – a distance of about 130 kilometres.

Out went the radio signal for success: "Ham and Jam, Ham and Jam". D-Day – the invasion of Normandy – had begun.

Countdown to invasion

The glider landings not only marked the start of D-Day; they also marked the end of four years of meticulous planning, begun at a time when it had seemed that Britain faced the might of Hitler's Nazi Germany alone. The disastrous defeat and subsequent evacuation of British troops from the French port of Dunkirk near the Belgian border in June 1940 marked a crisis point in the war in Europe. The troops had been caught in a tightening noose of Panzer divisions and Luftwaffe air strikes, a combination which had created a Nazi-occupied Europe. It was from this evacuation, however, that the idea grew that the only way to defeat Germany was to counter-attack.

But when? How? Who would do it? Where?

Britain's darkest hour

Four years earlier, in the dark days of 1940, a counter-attack had seemed impossible, but the idea had begun to form in the astute mind of the British Prime Minister, Winston Churchill. Since Dunkirk, Churchill had considered the possibility of invading "Fortress Europe" and striking at the heart of Germany – her capital, Berlin. But "Fortress Europe" was well defended and protected. The Atlantic Wall was a continuous line of concrete blockhouses, gun emplacements, barbed wire, mines and beach defences which followed the entire coast from Denmark to the Spanish border.

Britain could not hope to break the German hold on Europe without help. But after the Japanese attack on the American Pacific naval base at Pearl Harbor in December 1941, the United States entered the war and so Britain gained a powerful ally. It now seemed as though it just might be possible to mount a counter-invasion. The US President Franklin D. Roosevelt and Churchill met at Casablanca in January 1943 to assess the Allied resources which could be mustered for such an attempt. British Lt General F.E. Morgan, Chief of Staff to the Allied Supreme Commander, drew up what was to become known as the COSSAC Plan. After this, things moved quickly and at a conference in Teheran in December 1943 US General Dwight D. Eisenhower was chosen as Supreme Commander for the invasion.

Hope for the Allies

After the victory of the Allies in North Africa and the invasion of Sicily and Italy, Churchill wanted this Central Mediterranean campaign to be successfully completed before a north-west European front was opened up. His idea was that the two fronts would eventually combine in the sweep towards Berlin. But Roosevelt wanted an earlier invasion than this would allow and 1943 was his target date. In fact, the sheer enormity of the logistics – the organization of men, equipment, vehicles, ammunition and so on – ruled out the possibility of an invasion that soon.

As well as Eisenhower, other leaders were chosen for the mammoth undertaking which was to combine the Allies' land, sea and air forces. The operations of the Supreme Headquarters Allied Expeditionary Force – SHAEF – were directed from the centre of D-Day operations, Southwick House, near Portsmouth, by four men: Air Commander-in-Chief, Air Chief Marshal Sir Trafford Leigh-Mallory; Commander-in-Chief of the British Army Group, General Sir Bernard Montgomery, ("Monty", as he was popularly known); Naval Commander-in-Chief, Admiral Sir Bertram Ramsay; and Senior Commander of American Ground Forces, Lieutenant General Omar Bradley. The attack was to utilize two airborne and five seaborne divisions of British, American and Canadian forces, supported by men of the Free French, Dutch, Norwegian and Polish forces as well as Belgian, Czech, New Zealand, Australian and Rhodesian troops. This was to be the greatest seaborne invasion against the strongest coastal defences in the history of warfare.

Southwick House near Portsmouth, the centre for the D-Day operations.

Operation OVERLORD is mounted

In greatest secrecy, it was decided to mount the invasion on the northern coast of France, in Normandy. The codename for the invasion was to be Operation *OVERLORD*.

Vast resources would be needed, but the most important of these was a port through which the Allied invading forces could be supplied with vehicles, equipment and food. There were, of course, harbours on the Normandy coast, but most of these were just small fishing villages. The only suitable landing places were Le Havre and Cherbourg, but even if these were captured, the retreating Germans would make sure that the port facilities were mined or blown up to prevent the Allies from using them. It was Churchill who conceived the idea of building floating harbours in Britain and taking them across the Channel. He wrote a memo to Lord Mountbatten, Chief of Combined Operations: "Piers for use on beaches: They *must* float up and down with the tide. The anchor problem must be mastered . . . Let me have the best solution worked out. Don't argue the matter. The difficulties will argue for themselves."

But lack of ports was only one problem. Others included that of landing on unknown beaches. How soft was the sand? How deep was the water at high tide? At low tide? Secret trips were made at night by men in midget submarines, who brought back sand samples; geologists studied rock formations, and oceanographers deduced tidal flows. Aerial photographs were taken of the Normandy coast and a public appeal was put out for postcards and holiday photographs of any French beaches, as it was still a secret that Normandy was the target. Millions of pictures were sent in, but, of course, only those relating to Normandy were scrutinized in any detail.

The Atlantic Wall

In addition to the natural hazards there was the Atlantic Wall to contend with. Where exactly were the German batteries? How many were there? What types of gun did they contain? What kinds of mine had been laid in the sand? How formidable were the beach defences? What was the strength of the German forces in the area?

The preparations took far longer than expected. It soon became clear that to invade in 1943, as originally suggested,

German Commander Field Marshal Erwin Rommel inspecting beach defences of the Atlantic Wall in Normandy.

would be quite impossible. The earliest possible time for the invasion was 1944, as more tanks, ships, planes, landing craft and vehicles would have to be built first. Many of these would be made in the USA and shipped across the Atlantic in convoys. Machines based on conventional tanks and specially adapted for specific tasks, such as clearing mines from beaches before the troops could land, were also being experimented with. Because of their often cartoon-like appearance, these were called "Hobart's Funnies", after General Sir Percy Hobart who had developed the different designs. Troops had to be briefed about their objectives and trained to cope with getting in and out of landing craft while carrying kit and rifle in all kinds of weather conditions.

Long before D-Day, when the exact date was still to be decided, Allied commanders knew that they must have control of the air. The first military objective was to eliminate the German air force so that it would not be a danger to the thousands of troops landing on the beaches. It was also necessary to gain control of the shipping lanes across the Atlantic and clear them of German submarines, as it was from the USA that vital arms, vehicles and equipment would be brought.

By early 1944 the Luftwaffe had been effectively grounded and the shipping lanes made safe. The preparatory stages of OVERLORD were complete.

But what of the land forces? France was occupied by German forces who were moved around mainly by rail. The railways were therefore the next objective. The "interdiction programme" was the name given to the campaign undertaken by British bombers and members of the French Resistance to destroy or sabotage railway lines, bridges, tunnels, stations, marshalling yards and locomotive factories. They took the same action against German airfields, radar stations and canal and river bridges in France – anything to hinder the movement of German troops, especially along lines of communication leading to the beaches of Normandy. The aim was to isolate the battle area from the rest of France.

To prevent the Germans suspecting that Normandy was to be the site of the invasion, similar tactics were also carried out in the Pas de Calais, where the Germans expected any invasion to take place. The Allies encouraged them in this belief. They even left some radar stations there undamaged, to allow the Germans to pick up signals of a false invasion force heading towards the Pas de Calais.

Allied troops practising boarding landing craft via rope ladders from a troop carrier.

Combined operations training

Meanwhile, in a combined operation of army, air force, navy and Royal Marines, troops were being trained all over Britain, although most were in the West Country and Scotland. Men lived aboard troopships and practised such things as scrambling down nets slung over the ships' sides. They jumped into the tidal waters of Loch Fyne and other sites where the conditions were believed to resemble those on the Normandy coast. They endured forced marches in full battle kit, carrying rifles and ammunition in all weathers, day and night. They practised building Bailey bridges and pontoons. Some were stationed by an Ayrshire river which was similar to the River Orne in northern France – although, of course, the prospective invaders did not know that at the time.

As D-Day approached, troops were moved to camps close to ports such as Newhaven and Gosport, opposite the Normandy coast some 130 kilometres away across the English Channel. A "dress rehearsal" of seaborne and airborne forces was held on Slapton Sands in Devon. During this, some troops were killed when their craft were intercepted by undetected patrolling German E-boats. This incident was not made public until many years later.

As preparations for the big day became more intense, there were many small, secret commando raids – hit-and-run attacks on the Atlantic Wall which were intended to irritate the Germans, divert their attention and keep them guessing about the invasion.

Decoys and deceptions

Although German intelligence indicated that an Allied invasion was imminent, their reports of where and when it would occur were contradictory. The Allies intended to keep it that way. Elaborate and ingenious Allied deceptions fooled the German High Command into thinking that the invasion would be in the Pas de Calais. Movements of apparently large numbers of troops in East Anglia were faked. Dummy tanks, lorries and aircraft were built in the eastern counties. False radio messages were sent to imaginary army divisions. It was even arranged for Montgomery's "double" (an actor, Clifton James, who bore a striking resemblance to the commander) to be seen in the South East.

A fictitious 4th Army headquarters was "based" in Scotland. Training camps were set up, manoeuvres were carried out and wireless traffic relayed messages which indicated that an Allied invasion was aimed at German-occupied Norway. The idea was to discourage the Germans from withdrawing any of their forces from there.

A network of spies and double agents throughout Europe relayed vast amounts of information to German intelligence, much of it "planted" to deceive the Germans. One deception mounted in 1943 is known as "The Man Who Never Was". This involved obtaining the body of a young man who had recently died. He was given a new identity, that of a naval officer, and his body, carrying what looked like official secret Foreign Office documents, was put into the sea so that it would wash up on the Spanish coast and appear to be a casualty from a British submarine. As the Allies hoped, his body was recovered and his "secret" papers found their way to Berlin via German spies based in Spain. This was just one example of the complexity and attention to detail of the Allied decoy arrangements.

As D-Day approached, the weather forecasters were consulted almost hourly. Their predictions were not good – storms in the Channel. The Germans also took notice of their meteorologists, who said the same, and they concluded that there would be no invasion while these conditions prevailed. Having come to this conclusion, Field Marshal Erwin Rommel, Commander of the German 15th and 7th Armies

German Commander General Field Marshal Erwin Rommel.

(Army Group B), went home for his wife's brithday party.

At his headquarters near Paris, Commander-in-Chief for Germany's western forces, Field Marshal Gerd von Rundstedt, was also convinced that no invasion could take place in such bad weather. He was so confident that he even dismissed reports of the coded radio messages signalling the start of the invasion. He maintained that Eisenhower would hardly announce the invasion over the BBC radio!

D-Day was finally fixed for 5 June 1944.

Bad weather halts preparations

Men were transported from their camps. They boarded ships and landing craft. Some set off for the assembly area just off the south coast. Midget submarines had gone ahead to act as markers for the invading forces. Everyone was tense and alert but morale was high. The weather, however, continued to be bad, with storms and strong winds buffeting the coast, and so the invasion was postponed for 24 hours.

If the attack were delayed any longer morale would drop, the element of surprise would be lost, the weather might get

German Commander General Field Marshal Gerd von Rundstedt.

even worse, the tides would alter and there would be no moonlight to help the glider pilots and paratroopers. As it was, some men had been aboard the flat-bottomed landing craft in rough seas for two or three days, waiting for the signal to depart. They were already suffering from seasickness.

The coded "Invasion Imminent" message, the first verse of a poem by the nineteenth-century French poet, Paul Verlaine:

"Les sanglots longs
Des violons
De l'automne
Blessent mon coeur
D'une langueur
Monotone"

had been relayed to the French Resistance – *and* picked up by the Germans. As a result, the German 15th Army guarding the Pas de Calais had been put on alert; the 7th Army stationed in Normandy had not.

It was now or never – D-Day had to be 6 June 1944.

British troops embarking for the D-Day landings. Note the amount of equipment carried by each man and the camouflage on the helmets.

Under way

"OK, let 'er rip!"

Eisenhower's words launched one of the greatest gambles in military history – as great as those taken by Nelson at Copenhagen, Wellington at Waterloo and Napoleon in 1812. This was, however, a gamble in which the odds had been carefully stacked in the Allies' favour – at least in theory. But there was the bad weather to contend with.

Already midget submarines, towed part of the way across the English Channel by trawler, were heading for the Normandy beaches. There were dangerous rocky outcrops offshore and the submarines would act as markers for the invasion craft which were soon to follow. But no sooner had

X-class midget submarine which acted as one of the markers on the invasion beaches.

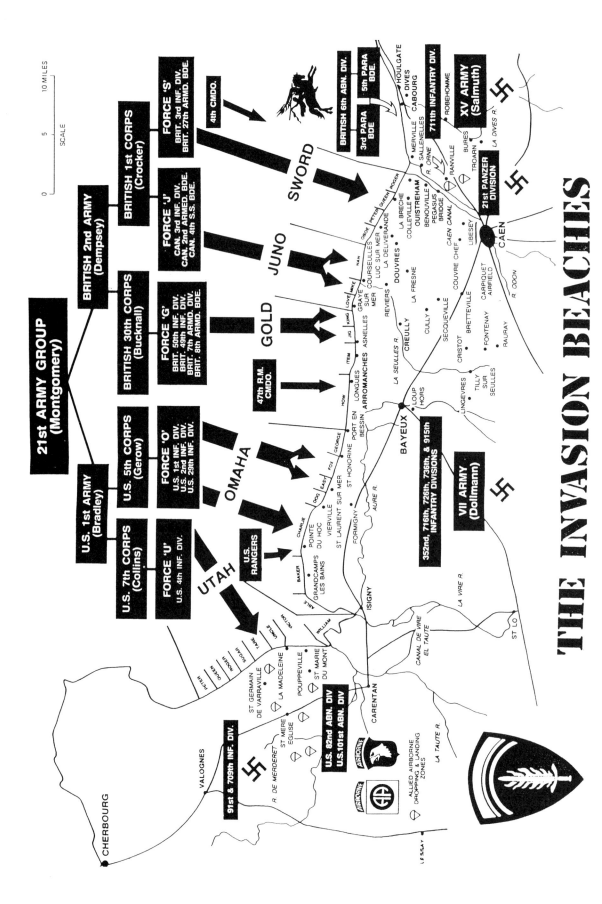

THE INVASION BEACHES

the submarines taken up their postions than they were told over the radio that D-Day had been postponed. They submerged and waited for further orders.

Other ships received the radio messages to stop and some even managed to return to port to mark time, but one large convoy somehow missed the signal and sailed on alone, straight for the Normandy coast, until it was found by British naval aircraft and told to turn back.

By evening, however, on 5 June, D-Day minus one, the invasion was under way. The waiting was over: the great armada of around 6,000 ships of all kinds assembled off the Isle of Wight, in an area so busy that it was jocularly known as Piccadilly Circus, and then headed east, apparently towards the Pas de Calais. But under cover of darkness the convoys of ships would separate into pre-arranged battle groups and turn south, instead, for Normandy. It was vital that the alteration in course should not be picked up by German radar stations, and so in the weeks before D-Day Allied bombers had jammed most of these or put them completely out of action. German coastal batteries, particularly those on the flanks of the invasion area, had also suffered bombardment from over 1,000 aircraft of RAF Bomber Command.

By nightfall the weather conditions had improved dramatically and the wind had eased. Throughout the night the seaborne assault force ploughed its way across the choppy waters of the English Channel. Battleships, anti-U-boat patrol boats, convoy escorts, tankers, hospital ships, cargo vessels, troop ships, flat-bottomed landing craft and a host of others carried men, supplies, guns, ammunition, tanks and vehicles which were chained to prevent them from sliding across the decks.

Planes were also heading towards the east and west flanks of the invasion area. Some carried paratroopers; others were towing gliders that carried airborne forces. From Caen to the Cotentin Peninsula the coast had been allocated to the British, the Americans and the Canadians. The British and Canadians would take the eastern half and the Americans the western half. The whole coastline had been divided into assault areas, each with a codename. The American invasion beaches were known as UTAH and OMAHA. The Canadians had been allocated JUNO, and the two British beaches were GOLD and SWORD.

Portsmouth News *map of the invasion beaches showing the assault forces in each area.*

False trails

While the *real* invasion force was crossing the Channel to
Normandy by both air and sea, other "invasion forces" were
heading towards the Pas de Calais. The first, codenamed
TITANIC, consisted of planes dropping dummy paratroopers, each "armed" with firecrackers timed to explode on
landing and sound like sporadic rifle fire. Another "airborne
invasion" was simulated by bombers dropping thousands of
strips of metal foil known as "window". On the screens of the
few remaining German radar stations, to the north-east of
Caen, this gave the impression of huge numbers of aircraft.
The Allies had carefully avoided bombing these radar
stations and left them intact so that they would be able to
detect and report to the German High Command the phoney
invasion fleet heading towards Calais.

Operations GLIMMER and TAXABLE were seaborne
"invasion fleets" of motor launches towing balloons contain-
ing radar reflectors and radar-jamming signals. They also
headed towards Calais, to increase the confusion as to the
location of the real invasion force.

No turning back

The British 6th Airborne Division headed towards the
eastern flank near Caen. Their objectives were the bridges
over the Caen Canal and the River Orne. H-Hour – the time
when the first paratroopers would jump – was 0020 hours.
The American 101st and 82nd Airborne Divisions aimed for
the Cotentin Peninsula on the extreme edge of the western
flank, and for them H-Hour was 0130 and 0230 hours
respectively. On arrival, they were to act as pathfinders and
mark out with flares the landing areas for the main invasion
force, which would be arriving by sea within hours.

The paratroopers had to clear the fields of "Rommel's
asparagus" – poles topped with mines designed to prevent
gliders from landing. They needed to secure and clear roads
leading from the invasion beaches, so that the invading troops
could push inland to gain a foothold. Enemy guns had to be
put out of action so that they could not be fired at troops
landing on the beaches. Bridges giving access to the beach
area had to be destroyed to prevent German troops stationed
inland from reinforcing the coastal defenders. And finally, a
bridgehead had to be established from which further
operations could be launched.

British and American bombers had left airfields in the south and south-west of England to bomb the coastal defences of Normandy. Bombing was to begin at 0315 hours and continue until 0500 hours. Rocket salvoes were to be fired from ships in the Channel to further "soften up" German resistance, that is, to destroy as many batteries and gun emplacements as possible and pave the way for the airborne and seaborne landings on the coast.

As the paratroopers, packed uncomfortably in their gliders, awaited the signal to begin the drop, below them, the real seaborne fleet was preceded by minesweepers clearing pathways through underwater mines. The invaders approached the French coast in darkness. Dawn was still an hour or two away. Landing and assault craft were lowered into the water from the large ships. Navy destroyers took up their positions to bombard the coast on the flanks of each invading brigade group. H-Hour was 0725 hours and 0745 hours for the British landing on the eastern beaches, and 0630 hours for US troops on the western beaches – times which had been carefully worked out to fit in with the tides.

There was no turning back now. Operation OVERLORD was under way.

Operation OVERLORD

Reports of American paratroopers landing in the Cotentin Peninsula south of Cherbourg were received by the German 7th Army stationed in that area without much apparent alarm. The Army was placed on alert, as a precaution. To the north-east, in the Pas de Calais area, the 15th Army had already been put on alert, German intelligence having deduced that the Paul Verlaine poem was broadcast to signal an imminent invasion.

The German Naval Group West agreed that the Allied operations were *not* the start of an invasion and so did not immediately send out naval patrols to investigate. The weather was still bad. The tides were unfavourable. It was not a good night for an invasion.

The 7th Army Headquarters reported to Rommel's Chief of Staff, General Hans Speidel, that "engine noises" could be heard out at sea in the English Channel and that one of the few remaining operative radar stations at Cherbourg had detected shipping activity. Speidel relayed this to von Rundstedt, but it was still thought to be nothing out of the ordinary.

At about 0300 hours on the morning of 6 June, German Admiral Kranke, Commander-in-Chief of the coastal defence system, became very suspicious. In spite of the bad weather, he ordered torpedo-boat flotillas to investigate the area between Le Havre and Cherbourg. After a brief skirmish with a British destroyer on the eastern flank of the Allied invasion force (although, of course, the Germans did not recognize it as such) the flotillas returned stating that there was "nothing to report".

German suspicions aroused . . . but reports discounted

With so many radar stations now out of action, the Germans found the lack of information worrying. Any information which was received was conflicting and misleading. Some of the Germans' confidence in the Atlantic Wall was beginning to crumble, with 74 out of the 92 radar installations from Holland to Cherbourg rendered ineffective by Allied bombing raids.

As the night dragged on, more and more reports reached

Rommel's Army Group B Headquarters at La Roche Guyon on the Seine. There were reports of airborne landings over a wide area, and later of heavy bombing. Just after 0600 hours, news came of the bombardment of the coast by Allied ships. Still the Germans considered it a feint, merely a diversionary tactic intended to draw their attention away from where they anticipated the real invasion would take place.

Field Marshal von Rundstedt, overall commander of the German forces in Western Europe, remained at his headquarters at St Germain-en-Laye near Paris. For various reasons, almost all the senior commanders of the 7th Army were absent from their stations during the early morning of 6 June. General Friedrich Dollman, commanding the German 7th Army, was on his way to Rennes in Brittany, with most of the divisional commanders. The German High Command had studied earlier Allied landings in the Mediterranean, all of which had been carried out in fine, calm weather. The Germans therefore saw this period as a respite during which they could stage exercises and manoeuvres in preparation for an invasion!

Rommel expected any invasion landing to be made at dawn, and on a high tide. He was sure that the best time for an Allied invasion had been in May, and that favourable conditions would not occur again until about 20 June. He felt confident that, for the time being at least, there would be no invasion and he welcomed this "breathing space". It was his wife's birthday. He took the opportunity to go home for a short leave to Herrlingen, near Ulm in Germany, with the idea also of trying to speak to Hitler at his mountain retreat at Berchtesgaden. He wanted to try to persuade Hitler to relinquish his personal control of the Panzer divisions within reach of the Normandy coast, so that they could come under the immediate supervision of the army.

Hitler had always believed that the invasion would be in Normandy, but with uncharacteristic tolerance he did not force his "hunch" and override the opinions of von Rundstedt, Rommel and others. There was often disagreement between Hitler and his generals, as he was always suspicious of them. He refused to delegate authority to them, or to trust them, and preferred to play off one against another. There was little agreement between the generals themselves and Hitler wanted to keep it that way. Despite Rommel's pleas he refused to hand over control of the crack Panzer divisions in Normandy.

Hitler was not told about the approaching Allied fleet and

airborne landings until it was obvious that something big was under way. He had been asleep, apparently feeling unwell, and no one had wanted to wake him and risk incurring his wrath with what might well prove to be a false alarm.

Allied luck holds

All this was, of course, most fortunate from the Allies' point of view – although they were not to know until much later of the German leaders' activities.

It had been Rommel's conviction that the only way to repel an invasion would be to hit the Allies on the beaches while they were landing and prevent their establishing a beachhead. He was reported to have said, ". . . the first twenty-four hours will be decisive . . . for the Allies, as well as Germany, it will be the longest day . . .". And now, with the invading forces dropping from the skies and approaching the beaches, he was not there!

News of the invasion reached Rommel at his home, by telephone, at 1030 hours – ten hours after the first Allied

German gun emplacement in concrete blockhouse on the Atlantic Wall.

airborne landings. "How stupid I was! How stupid I was!" he repeated over and over again. He hurried back to France, but the journey took half a day. He was not the only one who continued to believe that the Normandy attack was a decoy. Allied deceptions mounted in Operations TAXABLE, GLIMMER and TITANIC and the smokescreens in the Straits of Dover simply confirmed the Germans' idea that the real invasion would take place in the Pas de Calais.

In the confusion and indecision, the top Panzer divisions remained south of Chartres. They could not be moved north without direct orders from Hitler. Others, however, had been sent, after some delay, to counter-attack the British 6th Airborne Division in the east near Caen, and the US 82nd and 101st Airborne Divisions in the west in the Cotentin Peninsula.

When the Allied invasion fleet was first sighted at about dawn, the Germans were amazed. They had not believed the Allies had so many ships!

The German forces which were manning the concrete blockhouses of the Atlantic Wall, on watching the approaching fleet (almost 6,000 strong) and hearing the gunfire, bombing and naval bombardment, knew this was no phoney invasion. This was the real thing. But nothing seemed able to convince those in high command that this was *the* invasion, not just *an* invasion.

Landings

During the planning of the invasion of Normandy, Montgomery had outlined its aims. American forces were to capture Cherbourg, to give the Allies a port for bringing in further supplies. Then US armoured divisions were to break out from the Cotentin Peninsula, and swing south, then east, in a sweep towards Paris.

German armoured divisions would have to be prevented from moving in on the American front, and this would be the job of the British 2nd Army. They would need to secure all remaining ground communications so that German reserves and other forces could not reach the Cotentin Peninsula. It would also be vital to capture Caen on the first day of the invasion, thus directly threatening the road to Paris.

Before the invasion, Montgomery drew lines on the map, showing the points that each invading force – air, sea or land, British, Canadian or American – should have reached by midnight on D-Day.

Rommel and von Rundstedt also realized that Caen was a key city and kept their armoured divisions just to the south, ready to strike at either the Pas de Calais or Normandy. If the British captured Caen, these German armoured divisions would be effectively cut off from both coasts. The first objective of the Allied forces was, however, to secure the flanks of the invasion area, which were about 120 kilometres apart.

British airborne landings: 6th Airborne Division

Only a small party of the 6th Airborne Division stormed the bridges over the Caen Canal and the River Orne in the early hours of D-Day. Others of the division were landing elsewhere in the area. Their objectives were to clear the area of booby traps and mines in readiness for the arrival of reinforcements later in the day; to aid in holding the two bridges; to clear and secure Amfréville and Bréville which overlooked SWORD beach where the British 3rd Division would be landing at 0725 hours; and, lastly, to silence German batteries in the area which were set to fire on SWORD beach.

Not all were as lucky (or as expert) as Major Howard's glider pilot who landed within 50 metres of the goal – the Caen Canal bridge. Some gliders landed off target, missing the dropping zones by several hundred metres or more. Disorientated in the darkness, with no landmarks and no communications, as wirelesses often smashed on landing, many paratroopers lay low until dawn. Once it was light they were able to pick out landmarks such as the canal itself, and try to link up with their colleagues. However, any movement was likely to be spotted by German snipers, and machine-gun emplacements kept up rapid fire.

Out at sea the naval bombardment was in progress and eased the situation by putting some inland batteries out of action. Meanwhile, men of the 6th Airborne Division fought off repeated attacks and waited for the promised reinforcements. By mid-afternoon one brigade had arrived, together with three commando units. These included the 6th Commando, led by a Scottish piper, Bill Millin, whose bagpipes could be heard above the shooting. As darkness fell, at 2100 hours, two lines of aircraft, towing gliders and protected by fighter planes, came in low to the east of Caen, bringing the rest of the long-awaited reinforcements to the 6th Airborne Division.

US airborne landings: 101st Division

The 101st Airborne Division was to arrive at its allocated dropping zone from the west. After leaving bases in the south of England the gliders approached the Cotentin Peninsula in low cloud. Anti-aircraft fire unnerved the inexperienced pilots, who drifted off course so much that some of the equally inexperienced paratroopers were dropped as far as 8 kilometres from their target so that they were scattered over 35 kilometres. The primary objective for the paratroopers, following a concentrated landing, had been to secure the roads leading to UTAH beach. But as the paratroopers had been scattered, this seemed impossible.

The scattering, however, confused the Germans and gave them the impression that there were far more paratroopers than there really were. It also meant that the Germans could not identify a main body of troops.

During the planning of the invasion, Air Commander-in-Chief Leigh-Mallory had expressed doubts as to the feasibility of the parachute drops, saying that aircraft losses would be unacceptably high and that the area was a difficult one on which to land. But his objections had been overruled by Montgomery, who insisted that it was essential to stake a claim in the Cotentin Peninsula and isolate the port of Cherbourg as soon as possible. As it turned out, aircraft losses were not so very great, but Leigh-Mallory was proved right with regard to the problem of landing in such featureless countryside. It was a marshy area criss-crossed by dykes, ditches and hedges. Low-lying meadows between the Rivers Douve and Merderet had been flooded by the Germans, but from above looked like solid green fields. An 8-kilometre stretch of safe ground between these rivers was the dropping zone which has been allocated to the 101st Division.

The 101st's main goal was to capture the southernmost flank of UTAH beach to enable the seaborne US 4th Division, which would be landing at 0630 hours, to get inland. The paratroopers were to clear the five causeways running from the beach between the dunes, and to secure their inland exits so that assault troops could get a foothold. Another objective was to move south towards Carentan and destroy the bridges over the River Douve, but as the US troops were so scattered, this proved impossible. The 101st was to join up with the 82nd Division which had dropped to the west of them and the 4th Infantry Division (arriving by sea) in a closely combined air-sea operation. Out of 6,000 paratroopers dropped, however, only 1,000 actually managed to rendezvous.

Following a disastrous start, with paratroopers dropping in floods, minefields and even the sea, those troops who did manage to rendezvous were often separated from their units and so had to improvise, hitting secondary targets. They rallied under Major General Maxwell Taylor, commander of the 101st Division, who (unlike British commanders) jumped with his men in what he termed "intimate leadership". He and his men cleared the village of Pouppeville and captured the southernmost causeway. Eventually, during the course of the day, all five causeways and three German batteries were captured; fortunately, 50 American gliders landed exactly on target, and brought guns, ammunition and signal equipment.

The 101st did not manage to capture the bridges north of Carentan. Nevertheless, they harassed, skirmished, ambushed and sniped at German troops, causing great confusion. The German 91st Division and 6th Parachute Regiment had to fight to maintain their hold on the bridges. German communications were disrupted and German forces lured away from the coast, allowing the US 4th Infantry Division to land on UTAH beach and move inland.

US airborne landings: 82nd Division

The 82nd Airborne Division, under the command of Major General Matthew Ridgway, aimed to seize the bridges and causeways along the northern part of the Rivers Douve and Merderet. This was intended to prevent the Germans from counter-attacking from the west. It would also allow American invading forces to move westwards and inland.

One regiment, the 505th, was to land near and capture the little town of Ste Mère Eglise in order to command the main road to Cherbourg. They were also to capture the bridge over the Merderet to the west of the town and two others over the Douve on the southside. Two more regiments were to drop to the west of the Merderet, beyond the floods, and establish a bridgehead. Two hours after the first troops had landed, further guns and equipment were to be parachuted in. But this was not quite what happened.

One of the houses in the main square of Ste Mère Eglise had been hit by a stray incendiary bomb and was on fire. Occupying German forces lifted the curfew so that the townsfolk could fight the fire with water from the local pump using "chains" of buckets and improvised hoses. Suddenly, into all this activity, American paratroopers began dropping out of the night sky. Many became entangled in trees and telegraph wires or caught on roofs. There, they were immediately shot at by the German forces below. One paratrooper, John Steele, was caught on the tower of the church. By feigning death for several hours, he was lucky to escape with only an injured foot.

Other paratroopers were blown off course and landed amongst the billets of the German 91st Division, which was specially trained in anti-parachutist tactics. Others became mixed up with the 101st Division to the east. Others who landed in flooded areas drowned under the weight of their 50-kilogramme packs, or their parachutes dragged them down under the water. Not all were able to cut themselves free. Only one in 25 landed in the right place. Supplies dropped by parachute were lost or submerged so that they were rendered useless. As with the 101st, those who landed safely attempted to rendezvous, but many lost their bearings completely and wandered around for hours attempting to locate their units with the aid of little metal clickers with which they had been issued. If they received the correct pattern of "clicks" in response to a pre-arranged signal, they could safely emerge and rendezvous.

By 0400 hours, however, Ste Mère Eglise had been captured by American forces and the Stars and Stripes hoisted above the town. The bridges over the Merderet were not taken, as the Germans had already arrived by the time the American forces reached them, and so they were heavily defended. Nevertheless, the Americans managed to hold a base on the Cherbourg road which they had established earlier, and from there they harassed German troops. The 91st Division was pinned down for days, but this served some purpose since it diverted German troops from UTAH beach. One group of paratroopers, while taking cover behind a roadside hedge, saw an approaching vehicle which, as it grew closer, proved to be a German officer's car. After a moment's hesitation, one man sprayed it with a burst of machine-gun fire. As the car swerved, another threw a grenade at it before it crashed, killing all the occupants. Among these was Lt General Wilhelm Falley, Commander of the 91st Division. Other US paratroopers managed to put the 91st's headquarters out of action and so cut off communication with German High Command. It was not until six hours after the first troops had arrived on UTAH beach that the German High Command realized there had been any seaborne landings at all.

The American airborne landings seemed a complete disaster, with many casualties, but there were some strokes of luck for both the 82nd and the 101st Divisions, so that potential fiascoes turned into good fortune. Despite the Douve and Merderet bridges not being captured or destroyed, the paratroopers' efforts had not been in vain. They had achieved what Montgomery had planed, i.e. protected UTAH beach from German counter-attack from the south and west.

Although there was much confusion among American troops, that among the Germans was even greater. Their hesitations, delays and arguments gave the Allies much-needed time, while they were still trying to sort out the true invasion from the false. Panzer divisions were kept waiting for orders and in the meantime had to dodge Allied air attacks. Delay was to prove fatal to the Germans. Meanwhile, the Allied seaborne landings were under way.

Seaborne Landings

"Under the command of General Eisenhower, Allied Naval forces supported by strong air forces began landing Allied

Armies this morning on the Northern Coast of France."
(*Communiqué issued by General Eisenhower and broadcast
on the BBC by John Snagge on 6 June 1944*)

The Normandy coast had been divided up into five invasion
areas which were named UTAH, OMAHA, GOLD, JUNO
and SWORD. Each beach was divided into small sections,
each of which was under the command of a beachmaster, who
directed operations in his area.

Timing of the landings was crucial, since every man's fate
depended upon everyone being in the right place at the right
time. But the most important factor to be taken into
consideration was the sea. Rising tides began in the west.
Each seaborne assault had to be timed to coincide with the
tide on that particular area of coast. UTAH, the beach
furthest west, was therefore the first to be invaded.

UTAH Beach

On UTAH Beach, H-hour (the time when the first landing
craft would come ashore) was at 0630 hours. The invading
force here was the US 4th Infantry, whose orders were to

*A DUKW ("Duck")
amphibious vehicle leaving
an LST (Landing Ship Tank)
for the run-in to the
invasion beach. Note other
ships of the invasion fleet in
the background.*

advance inland from the beach along the five causeways between the dunes (already secured by the 101st Airborne Division) and link up with the 82nd Airborne Division. Together, they were to clear the main roads and establish a bridgehead over the River Vire.

Before all this could happen the seaborne assault force 20 kilometres out in the English Channel had had to be manoeuvred. The fleet, which included the USS *Nevada* and other American and British cruisers, had assembled at 0200 hours. All the ships anchored in previously arranged positions. Large troopships had lowered flat-bottomed assault craft into the water, and loaded into them the infantry battalions which were to lead the attack. Amphibious landing craft – "Ducks" (DUKWs), duplex drive tanks (DDs) and landing ship tanks (LSTs) – were unloaded closer to the shore, escorted by motor torpedo boats (MTBs), mine-sweepers and escort destroyers.

The sea here was fairly calm, as UTAH beach was in the lee of the Cotentin Peninsula. Nevertheless, the troops were already cold, wet and seasick. Once in the assault craft, they still had over an hour to wait before the run-in to the beach. There were some casualties caused by undetected minefields at sea as well as by the inevitable collisions. Men fell overboard, and were crushed on scramble netting. Those who fell into the sea drowned, as they were pulled under by the weight of their packs. One DD tank hit a mine and was thrown 30 metres into the air. The noise was added to by the naval bombardment overhead.

In spite of these difficulties, everything seemed to be going according to plan until bad luck struck the first wave of invading troops. A sudden, surprisingly strong current carried the whole fleet too far south to a position opposite the Pouppeville causeway, and left them unsure of what was the best thing to do. Should they try to return to where they should have been, stand firm where they were, or push inland from that point and establish a beachhead almost unopposed?

Fortunately, those who had landed included the 57-year old veteran Brigadier General Theodore Roosevelt (a descendant of the former US President of the same name). He assessed the situation quickly. Alternately cheering on and calming down the troops, he acted as an impromptu beach-master, directing the landing battalion to head inland, leaving the beaches clear for the troops following. His action proved to be successful. Three hours later, fifteen waves of US assault troops were ashore with vehicles, track-laying equipment and arms. Most were still close to the beach, but the early invaders were advancing steadily into the countryside.

Those troops still in the beach area were within range of the German battery to the east of Pointe du Hoc – an almost sheer cliff face rising out of the sea. The battery dominated that part of the coastline, and threatened UTAH and OMAHA beaches; therefore it had to be put out of action. The US 2nd Rangers (commandos) were assigned to scale the cliffs. Using rope ladders, rope-trailing rockets, grapnel hooks, and even ladders from the London Fire Brigade and hand-holds cut into the 30-metre high cliff face, they doggedly made their way up. The German defenders fought back with small-arms fire and hand grenades, and also used axes to cut the climbing ropes. Only 90 of the 225 men who began the ascent survived, but they finally succeeded in overrunning the battery – only to find no big guns there after all! By chance, a two-man patrol found the guns and ammunition further inland, well hidden but totally unguarded.

Meanwhile, back on the beaches, the obstacles to invasion were cleared fairly quickly. The main problem was congestion, which grew worse as more men and vehicles were landed. It had to be cleared quickly to enable troops to push inland and link up with the 82nd Airborne Division. Their next aim was to capture the Douve and Merderet bridges.

What were the Germans doing during this time? As a result of Allied naval and aerial bombing, combined with sabotaging of railway and telephone lines by the French Resistance, there was almost no communication between the headquarters of the German 84th Corps and the German coastal defences. The RAF attacked the armoured divisions of the 7th Army, and prevented them from reaching the beaches. At midday the German commanders at headquarters still knew nothing about landings on UTAH beach. Even if they had known what was going on, they had no troops left to send as reinforcements. Their reserves were already in the field trying to contain the main body of paratroopers of the 101st, who had diverted their attention away from UTAH beach. Others were attempting to counter-attack the British and Canadians who had landed further east.

Despite some anxious moments, the UTAH beach landings had gone virtually according to plan. Thanks to good luck, together with sheer determination on the part of hitherto green troops, the US 4th Infantry Division had lost only 197 men. But just a little further east along the coast, on OMAHA beach, events were not running so smoothly.

OMAHA Beach

For the 1st and 29th Infantry Divisions of the US 5th Corps on OMAHA beach, H-hour was also 0630 hours. Their aim was to infiltrate four narrow valleys that led inland from the beach, then to link up with the US 4th Infantry Division which had landed on UTAH beach.

The landings on OMAHA beach were affected by misfortune, however. Low cloud meant that aerial bombing was ineffective. The naval bombardment was started too late to successfully "soften up" the defenders. Finally, USS *Nevada*'s guns created so much smoke and haze that her gunners overshot their targets because they could not see them. To add to this, the coastline here presented the most unsuitable terrain of all the landing sites, as it had alternating strips of soft sand and marsh, a steep shingle belt, off-shore rocks, a concrete seawall and steep bluffs. Man-made obstacles were mines, barbed wire, booby traps and anti-personnel mines on top of the bluffs. The whole beach was under constant German observation and cross-fire from either side. As well as all this, the 716th German Coastal Defence Division was backed up by the tough, experienced 352nd Division, which was on full-scale practice in the area.

Allied troops were at a disadvantage before they even reached the shore as OMAHA beach lacked the protection of the Cotentin Peninsula. It was swept by waves over a metre high, gusting winds and strong currents. Darkness and sea-sickness made matters worse still. There was a very long run to the shore after troops had been transferred to the landing craft 20 kilometres out to sea. Many of the the landing craft were swamped or capsized so that DD tanks, guns and vehicles were lost and the infantry coming ashore lacked

US troops going ashore. Packs, wirelesses, boxes, rifles and other equipment are carried by each man.

armoured support. Many troops landed in the wrong places, and units were mixed up.

As the first men approached the beach, German machine-guns opened fire. Bullets ricocheted off the ramps of the landing craft and killed men as they climbed out into the water. Others missed their footing, fell and were drowned under the weight of their packs. Others simply shed their packs and ran on. Over three-quarters of the wirelesses which had been issued were abandoned because they were too heavy. As a result, American troops were left with few means of communication.

As men, vehicles and equipment landed in quick succession, a bottleneck resulted because they accumulated on the beach faster than they could move inland. Wrecked tanks were stranded, some vehicles refused to start after their soaking in the sea, many were set on fire by direct hits, and the crews of some were killed. Stretcher bearers attempted to rescue the wounded. German beach obstacles had to be removed; debris was washed ashore and littered the beaches.

Paths had to be cleared to allow men and vehicles in the next wave of assault craft to land. This took time and delay made matters worse. The tide came in fast. As the Americans had refused to use Hobart's "Funnies" to clear paths through the beach defences, they had only bulldozers and engineers. Because of this, half the engineers were killed and only 2 out of the 16 bulldozers got beyond the beach. The amphibious tanks were not designed to withstand prolonged battering by heavy seas, and so only five out of 32 managed to cross the beaches.

The first American troops to land were trapped on the 6-kilometre stretch of beach. Others followed in quick succession, and the beach rapidly became congested. In the chaos which soon arose, it became a case of every man for himself as far as crossing the beach was concerned. Some gave up completely; others dug in, fled back to the sea, sheltered behind vehicles on the beach or ran blindly forward. The number of wounded rose rapidly. Nevertheless, small groups of men began to scramble up the bluffs, dodging enemy fire as they climbed. They mounted a head-on attack against the enemy fortifications which guarded the beach and the lanes that led inland.

The situation became easier when British and US destroyers came close to the shore and bombarded the German gun positions. Within an hour and a half of the first (apparently disastrous) landings, some troops had managed to reach the top of the bluffs. They forged inland, over-running German gun emplacements as they advanced towards the villages of Vierville and St Laurent. They were stopped before they had penetrated 4 kilometres inland, however. The German 352nd Division put up strong resistance and there was street fighting in the fortified villages.

Meanwhile, OMAHA Beach was still under heavy fire. It became known as "bloody OMAHA" because there were over 3,000 casualties. It was the most precarious of the D-Day beaches, but during the ordeal the experienced US 1st Division bolstered the confidence of the untried 29th Division.

The American generals placed a great deal of confidence in the dash and courage of their infantrymen, but these qualities were insufficient to overcome the hazards of OMAHA beach. This over-confidence, combined with a lack of tactical caution, almost led to disaster. Offshore on the USS *Augusta* Lt General Bradley wondered whether it would be best to abandon the men on OMAHA beach, and to follow up just the UTAH beach landings and help the British and Canadians in the eastern sector. But the American General Huebner had assessed the situation. He called a halt to all further landings until the equipment, vehicles, debris and men were cleared from the beaches. He then sent in extra combat troops and ordered a further naval bombardment. When added to the determination of small groups of American soldiers who refused to be beaten and pushed inland skirmishing, sniping and destroying pillboxes as they went, these measures began to turn the tide. Finally, enough men to create a self-sufficient fighting force filtered through

Members of a US landing party helping their comrades ashore from a life raft.

and began to link up. Soon after 1300 hours the balance was tipping, albeit very slightly, in the Americans' favour.

There was some good fortune for the Americans, however. Six hours after the first landings on OMAHA beach, the Chief of Staff of the German 352nd Division had prematurely informed von Rundstedt that his division had "thrown the invaders back into the sea". Furthermore, believing the invaders on OMAHA beach to have been virtually wiped out by midday, and unaware of the landings on UTAH beach, he sent more than half his reserves against the British 50th Division, which had broken through the Atlantic Wall in the eastern invasion area. His remaining battalions were involved in trying to eject the Americans from Vierville and St Laurent and also to dislodge the 2nd Rangers from Pointe du Hoc. He therefore had no troops left to send to OMAHA beach.

GOLD Beach

GOLD Beach was the British beach furthest to the west, allocated to the 50th Division of the 3rd Corps. H-hour here was at 0725 hours. Two midget submarines, sent out earlier, marked the edges of the assault area. A protracted naval bombardment, lasting longer here than on the American landing beaches, helped in the "softening up" process. HMS *Ajax* was able to silence unaided, within 20 minutes, the battery of big guns west of Arromanches.

The weather here was as bad as at OMAHA Beach, and led to similar accidents. On the whole, however, despite the rough weather, things went well on GOLD Beach. The atmosphere was in contrast to the grimness and tension of the inexperienced troops landing on the American beaches. A gramophone could even be heard playing "Roll out the Barrel!".

The German stronghold of Le Hamel, which was manned by troops of the 352nd Division, was cut off from other units. Although they fought bravely they were unable to pin down the British and prevent them from establishing a foothold out of range of the German guns.

The men of the Green Howards established themselves on a ridge three kilometres inland, only two hours after landing, and by the end of the day had penetrated 10 kilometres inland. They managed to link up with the Canadians on JUNO Beach. The members of several units of the 50th Division and "Desert Rats" of the 7th Armoured Division were full of momentum and they were clear of the beaches by 1100 hours, sweeping all before them as they fought their way inland to the Caen-Bayeux road and even to the outskirts of Bayeux itself. They were only three kilometres short of the position marked by Montgomery as the one they should aim to reach by the end of D-Day.

However, all did not go according to plan for the 47th Royal Marine Commandos, who were caught on beach obstacles under heavy fire. Even so, their thorough training paid off. Casualties were so light that the medics were able to spend part of their time unloading ammunition. Eventually the Marine Commandos also managed to clear the beaches.

The 50th Division secured a beachhead, and the organization worked smoothly. Troops, equipment, vehicles and stores were brought ashore. The little port of Arromanches was captured and became the base for the portable harbours, code-named "Mulberries", whose concrete sections were towed across the Channel and assembled nearby.

The German counter-attack was initially a hit-and-miss affair, as most units had been taken by surprise. Some troops were brought to the scene by bicycle, their only available means of transport. They were under constant air attack from the RAF's Spitfires and Hurricanes, which also fired on roads, railways, ammunition dumps and petrol stores, which were blown up in the effort to prevent German troops moving towards the coast.

JUNO Beach

H-hour on JUNO Beach was between 0735 and 0745 hours. This beach had been designated as part of the British 1st Corps landing area, the rest of which was SWORD Beach to the east. JUNO Beach was allotted to the 3rd Canadian Division and the 2nd Canadian Armoured Brigade, which formed part of the British 1st Corps. Their goal was

British infantry wade ashore with bicycles for transportation in France.

Carpiquet airfield, 18 kilometres inland, to the west of Caen. The weather conditions here were as bad as on OMAHA Beach and for a time it looked as though there might be a repetition of the same initial setbacks.

At the mouth of the River Seulles the tides and reefs were dangerous and German defences were strong. There was, however, only a short run-in across the beach, which had the added advantage of a little shelter from the dunes. But cloud cover made Allied bombing inaccurate and caused naval gunners to overshoot their targets.

Canadian troops were renowned for their dash and verve. They were also strongly motivated, as they felt they were avenging the 3,000 Canadian casualties which had occurred during the frontal assault on Dieppe in 1942. After a brilliant attack on the beaches, against all odds, the Canadians stormed the villages of Bernières and Courseulles. Here they encountered opposition and engaged in house-to-house and street fighting before they were able to move further inland. Inevitably, they eventually began to run out of steam and, as beach clearance slowed, the advance inland flagged. Reserves found themselves stuck on the beaches and unable to follow up the first wave of assault troops, and therefore unable to take Caen by nightfall. Allied tanks moved along the Caen-Bayeux road until darkness fell. By this time they were within reach of the suburbs but, as they were without infantry support, they had to pull back and wait.

As the day passed there were more hold-ups both on the beach and in Bernières. The Germans had dug in near Bény-sur-Mer, but were cleared out by mid-afternoon. This released the accumulated men and vehicles on the beach and allowed the troops to advance inland from Bernières. Even so, there was still a large entanglement of Canadian troops to be sorted out and by the time this was cleared the initial impetus was lost. Nonetheless, they forged 11 kilometres inland – the best advance achieved from any of the beaches – and managed to link up with the British 50th Division from GOLD Beach. They were only just short of their objective – the Carpiquet airfield. This was strongly defended, and was to remain so for four weeks.

Inadequate tank support was aggravated as the Germans, entrenched in fortified houses and villas in the village of Langrune, destroyed leading tanks and pinned down the Commandos. A small section of coastline remained in German hands and so protected Douvres, just inland. This was the site of one of the few remaining operational radar stations which remained in touch with the German 84th Corps HQ.

At the end of the day the 21st Panzers moved north through Caen and engaged the British 3rd Division and the Canadians. German troops even made their way through to the coast. The Allied beachhead might have been divided but for the arrival of further members of the British 6th Airborne Division, who brought reserves and equipment in 250 gliders. While low-flying RAF planes machine-gunned German gun positions, 249 gliders got through and joined up with those members of the 6th Airborne Division who had landed there in the early hours of the morning.

While the Germans hesitated, the Allies closed the gap in their defences once and for all.

SWORD Beach

SWORD Beach was the invasion beach furthest to the east. H-hour here was at 0725 hours, and it was the landing area for the British 3rd Division. They had been set the tasks of capturing Caen, 16 kilometres inland, and getting reinforcements to the British 6th Airborne Division, which had been holding out on the eastern flank of the invasion area since just after midnight. These reinforcements were to hold this area against possible counter-attack by German troops stationed in the Pas de Calais.

German beach defences here were particularly strong, as villas and houses had been turned into small fortresses. Big German guns at Le Havre could fire on SWORD Beach, but in the event they were largely ineffective, because smokescreens prevented them from sighting their targets. These smokescreens did, however, help the German navy make its only effective strike of the day: an MTB (motor torpedo boat) flotilla, having penetrated a smokescreen at about 0330 hours, saw the invasion fleet and opened fire. The

HMS Warspite *in action off Normandy. Note that one of the rear turret guns has been put out of action in an earlier engagement.*

Medics tend the wounded brought to a field dressing station by stretcher bearers.

warships HMS *Ramilles*, HMS *Warspite* and HMS *Largs* narrowly avoided being hit by torpedoes. The Norwegian destroyer, *Svenner*, was hit and sunk before the German MTBs returned to port.

Many men in the British 3rd Division were veterans of the Dunkirk evacuation of 1940 and, like the Canadians, were eager for revenge. Like the men on GOLD Beach, they went into battle to the sound of Scottish pipes, a bugle salute and a rendering of a speech from Shakespeare's *Henry V*.

Inevitably, however, there were casualties. The dead were draped side by side over the seawall. The wounded were treated in field dressing stations and many were returned to England on hospital ships. By 0930 hours the South Lancashires, with tank support, were almost three kilometres inland at Hermanville. Other villages and small towns such as Riva Bella, Colleville-sur-Orne and Ouistreham were steadily cleared, the last by jubilant Free French forces. Commandos fought their way inland to reinforce the men who had made early morning glider landings.

SWORD Beach. Note the clutter of vehicles, equipment, beach defences and debris.

French commandos who landed on D-Day being greeted by villagers in Amfréville.

Some regiments could not keep up the early impetus sufficiently to advance immediately to Caen. They therefore dug in – just eight kilometres from their objective. The King's Shropshire Light Infantry moved on, however, and came to within four kilometres of Caen by 1600 hours. They dug in at Libesey, on the outskirts of the town, to prepare for a possible tank attack the following day, but then the Germans approached from the south. The area was continuously shelled and mortared, in addition to being heavily mined. It was here that the skill and courage of the Royal Engineers were stretched to the utmost as they cleared the ground of booby traps and explosives. In the late afternoon some 21st Panzer Division tanks counter-attacked from the Caen area – too late to repel the Allied invasion, but still in time to hold Caen. Other German tanks engaged at Ranville, further east, met with stiff resistance from a quickly-established Allied gun line.

For the Germans it was too late. The tanks could not get through the British line, let alone push it back to the coast. But those few German tanks did succeed in holding Caen, for the time being at least. To the Allies, Caen was almost within grasp – so near, yet so far.

Beach landings – success for the Allies

Everywhere Hobart's "Funnies" were invaluable, clearing the beaches of mines and booby traps and paving a safe way ashore with their flails, track-layers and "carpet rolls" (described on page 47). They were also able to give the assault troops covering fire and had within a short time cleared gaps in the beach obstacles and minefields, allowing troops to move inland. On all beaches tanks, vehicles and men accumulated on the narrow shoreline and so, because of incessant German shelling, many casualties were incurred.

The use of Hobart's "Funnies" on the British beaches meant that the death-rate was less than might have been expected. This was in contrast to the very heavy casualties on OMAHA Beach, where American commanders had scorned the use of such devices.

On all beaches except SWORD Beach, the sea was too rough for most of the specially adapted, waterproofed (DD) tanks to "swim" ashore. They had to be brought in "dry" on landing craft, and consequently were unable to give covering fire to the infantry. Some were lost through being swept back on mines and beach obstacles.

Frogmen managed to defuse some underwater mines which had been covered by the fast-approaching high tide. Even so, many craft were swamped, sunk or blown up, especially when returning to the ships from the beaches. The debris clogged up the shore, and some further landings had to be delayed while space was cleared for follow-up troops and vehicles to land.

Without back-up support of man- and fire-power, the Atlantic Wall was crumbling. There was little chance for the Germans to regroup or call for swift reinforcements in what had turned out to be a race between the British and the 21st Panzers to see who could get to Caen first. Any German troop movement was spotted from the air by Allied planes, and strafed. The 21st Panzers eventually managed to move north towards Caen, but by then it was evening, and so too late. It was the defenders who were battered, surprised, caught off-guard, disorganized and suffering under divided leadership. Despite the earlier mixture of good and bad luck on the invasion beaches, by evening fortune appeared to favour the invaders. The objective had been achieved. The Allies had thrown a cordon round German movements in the Cotentin Peninsula by breaking 10 kilometres into Fortress Europe. By midnight on D-Day they held a 36-kilometre front.

Rommel had missed his chance of stopping the invasion on the beaches.

THE INVESTIGATION

Why Normandy?

In 1944 the Axis powers controlled every country in Western Continental Europe except Sweden, Switzerland and Spain, which were neutral. The Axis countries believed themselves to be well protected by the Atlantic Wall, which ran from Denmark to Spain, and easily able to repel an invasion. The Allies considered that an Anglo-American invasion of France – a counter-attack – was an essential element in the defeat of Nazi-dominated Europe. But they knew that an ill-prepared, hastily organized invasion would fail. An earlier raid at Dieppe in 1942 had incurred severe losses and proved only that it was virtually impossible to take a well-defended port by a head-on attack.

What happened before D-Day? In May 1943 German forces under Rommel had been driven out of North Africa. The Allies had gone on to invade Sicily, which fell in August 1943, and then launched an invasion of Italy. This was a three-pronged attack across the Straits of Messina, Taranto and Salerno, and took place during the first week of September 1943. It was seen as an attack on the "soft underbelly" of Europe.

The decision to invade Italy was arrived at despite disagreement among Allied Commanders. There were already plans for an invasion of north-west Europe in the following year, and it was thought by some that a move into Italy might detract from this main Allied attack. However, the earlier invasion achieved its objectives: to knock the Italian army out of the war; and to gain possession of the airfield at Foggia, east of the Appennines, for use in Allied operations against southern and eastern areas of Germany. (The north and west of Germany already suffered continual bombing raids carried out from British bases.) This campaign continued throughout 1943 and into the summer of 1944. It effectively diverted twenty Axis divisions which would otherwise have been used on the Russian Front or against Allied troops invading north-west Europe.

Several countries in the Eastern Mediterranean, such as Greece and Yugoslavia, despite being overrun by Germany, had guerilla Resistance movements. They were aided by Allied forces, who secretly dropped supplies, equipment, ammunition and men. Early in 1944 there was hope that the combined efforts of partisans, the various Resistance movements and Allied military forces would gradually encircle the Axis forces in Europe.

By attacking the Axis Powers on all fronts, the Allies hoped to stretch German forces to the limit, so that an Allied thrust into north-west Europe would see the final defeat of Germany.

The Russian view   For some time, Stalin had been pressing for the establishment of a second front to divert German forces away from the Russian front. He did not regard the Anglo-American operation in North Africa and the invasion of Sicily as establishing a "proper" front, despite the fact that Germany had to move several crack divisions away from Russia to fight in the Mediterranean.

When, therefore, the original date for D-Day was set at 1 May 1944, perhaps with more political than military consideration, it re-established understanding between the Allies. Stalin was reassured by Roosevelt's promise to create a second front. There was still disagreement, however, as Roosevelt favoured a French second front, while Churchill wanted to put it off until the Italian campaign had succeeded. He wanted Allied troops in France to be able to link up with those fighting their way north through Italy in order to roll up the western front and form a concerted drive to Berlin.

Where, when and how?   The first task facing the COSSAC planners was to decide on the best area for an invasion. This decision was limited by the capacities of the Allied air, sea and land forces: ultimately, it was the limitations of aircraft which roughly defined the possible area. The extent of an aircraft's flight was determined by the amount of fuel it could carry in its tanks. This was known as the "operational range". Heavy bombers, such as the B-17 "Flying Fortress" of the US Air Force, had a longer operational range, and so could hit targets further afield, than smaller fighting planes. Most of the aircraft used against coastal targets, for reconnaisance and for fighter operations, were the Spitfires and Hurricanes of the RAF. A

Spitfire could only carry enough fuel to enable it to cross the channel, attack a target and return (a total distance of 320-400 kilometres). This was, therefore, the limiting factor. The invasion area had to be set within this radius from the south and south-east of England in order for these aircraft to give covering fire to invading troops.

Naval requirements also imposed constraints. Their main need was an area sheltered from summer gales and high seas, as these were prevalent in the Channel, even in summer, because of weather fronts moving in from the Atlantic. Allied naval forces would have to protect the landing troops against surface and underwater attack and for this would need convenient and relatively calm waters.

The army's requirements were a little less rigid. They needed good, firm landing beaches with easy access to flat, open land in order to assemble equipment, troops, tanks and guns.

When the requirements of the three forces were combined, only four possible areas remained: southern Holland-Belgium, the Somme estuary, the Seine estuary and Pas de Calais, and Normandy. The first of these was unsuitable because the network of canals and dykes in the hinterland would impede the movement of troops. The Somme estuary was too narrow for an Allied advance on a wide front and it was also divided by a river. The Seine estuary and Pas de Calais were known to be the areas most heavily defended by coastal artillery, which might have a devastating effect on Allied ships trying to protect assault troops. In addition, the Allies knew that the Germans considered this the most likely invasion site. That left Normandy – the stretch of coast between the Cotentin Peninsula and the River Orne. In Normandy coastal defences were less well developed than further east, and the terrain itself met most of the requirements, although in certain areas it was by no means easy. Naval leaders knew that the only area which could offer protection was leeward of the Cotentin Peninsula: the Normandy coast. Despite its being almost 160 kilometres from southern English ports, the area had important advantages. It was within easy reach of the sheltered Brittany harbours to the west, and, from a long-term point of view, Normandy had a large inland area where troops could be given a rest, vehicles could be massed and organized, airstrips could be laid and supply bases and ammunition dumps established for future use. All this could be contained between the natural boundaries of the Seine and Loire with a minimum of defence forces.

The choice is made   The main disadvantage of Normandy was the countryside, with its small woods and fields and high-banked sunken lanes topped by hedges, known as *"bocage"*. In places there were swampy areas cut by dykes, and also stone-built farms, which offered perfect cover for German snipers. But while this would hinder the movement of Allied troops, vehicles and tanks, it was also unsuitable terrain for the kind of large-scale Panzer attacks that might have devastated the invaders.

Normandy had fewer German airfields than the Pas de Calais, but many flat areas which would be suitable for use by the Allies. Once the ground was cleared of the anti-glider/aircraft devices known as "Rommel's asparagus", the Allies could use bulldozers to create landing strips.

Normandy was the area that the Germans considered the least likely site for an Allied invasion. It was the furthest from the British bases; it had no ports; and the tides and terrain were different from those the Allies had experienced during previous landings in North Africa, Sicily and Italy. Consequently, German coastal defences here were lighter than in the Pas de Calais, and the defence forces stationed here tended to be small bodies of less experienced troops. The Allies had the element of surprise – no mean advantage.

At the planning stage, the COSSAC command were unanimous in their choice of Normandy. Later, air force leaders, especially the Air Commander-in-Chief, Leigh-Mallory, had reservations, as they believed that airborne losses would be too heavy. In the event, however, they were proved wrong.

How did the Allies prepare for D-Day?

In order to put Operation OVERLORD into action according to plan, the Navy needed an additional 150 mine-sweepers, 240 warships and 1000 landing craft. These were supplied, somewhat reluctantly, by the US Navy Pacific Fleet. Because this transfer took time, the original D-Day date was postponed from 1 May to June. Although there were enough trained paratroopers for the airborne landings to secure the flanks of the invasion areas, there were not enough glider pilots to take them to the designated sectors, and so more had to be trained. This also took time.

Extra tanks and other vehicles had to be built and shipped across the Atlantic from American factories to add to those being built in Britain. Scores of British towns held fund-raising events to pay for extra aircraft; some "adopted" a ship or a plane and sent money to pay for it.

Ready to embark for Normandy, two types of Hobart's "Funnies" are the "flail tank" (note the flail, covered during sea voyage), and two "fascine tanks".

Hobart's "Funnies"   Work was done on special equipment to clear mines and booby traps from the landing area, and the experimental devices were tried out on British beaches. Some, such as a huge remote-controlled, bobbin-shaped device for clearing pathways through mines and barbed wire entanglements, proved to be uncontrollable and so were abandoned. Others, based on conventional Churchill tanks and developed for different terrains and uses by Colonel (later General Sir) Percy Hobart, were much more successful. The "fascine tank" carried bundles of wooden palings to fill in shell holes and improvise as ramps against walls so that the tank could move over these obstacles. "Carpet-layers" carried canvas on a huge roll on the front of the tank and laid this over soft clay areas to prevent the tank sinking. "Flail tanks" had drums *Types of Hobart's "Funnies"*   mounted on the front: these rotated and hurled chains laced

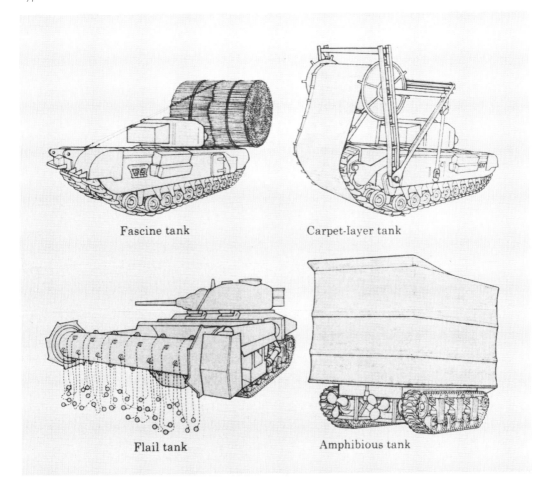

Fascine tank

Carpet-layer tank

Flail tank

Amphibious tank

with weights against the ground to explode mines. "Crocodiles" were modified Churchill tanks which towed trailers of flame fuel. From these they threw sheets of fire into enemy-held trenches and positions 50 metres ahead of invading forces. DD tanks were shrouded in canvas and provided with propellers to make them amphibious and so able to be unloaded at sea. This meant that they could drive ashore and land at the same time as the infantry, giving much-needed covering fire.

All these devices, with the possible exception of the DD tanks, which could not be used to their full potential in heavy seas, were to prove invaluable to the invading forces. In addition to the armoured vehicles built specially for the Normandy landings, other equipment was adopted, adapted or converted from civilian vessels. Amphibious troop carriers known as "Ducks" (DUKWs – Duplex Drive Amphibious Trucks), which had been used successfully in North Africa, Sicily and Italy, would once more prove their worth.

Mulberries and gooseberries

There remained the problem of harbours. The Germans held Cherbourg, and would put it out of action when they retreated. The Allies knew that they could not hope to capture a harbour suitable for landing follow-up troops and supplies. The solution was provided by do-it-yourself, prefabricated harbours, called "Mulberry" harbours, made of concrete caissons (floating structures which, when fixed in place, kept the sea from flooding the harbour under construction). There were to be two Mulberries: one for the British and one for the Americans. Each was approximately the size of Dover harbour. There were also piers or jetties which were to be erected just off the coast, near the small ports of Arromanches and Port-en-Bessin.

Obsolete ships, known as "gooseberries", were to steam out across the Channel under their own power and would then be sunk in line, bow to stern, with concrete caissons to form an outer breakwater. Within this breakwater was an area protected from the weather. Running from the inner harbour, there were long flexible roadways on pontoons, which floated up and down with the tide. These were made from flat-bottomed boats, bolted together, and over which metal plates were laid to form bridges strong enough to take the heaviest vehicles ashore. Deeper-draught vessels could anchor on the seaward side of the blockships (old ships which had been sunk in line to act as a block against the sea) in the

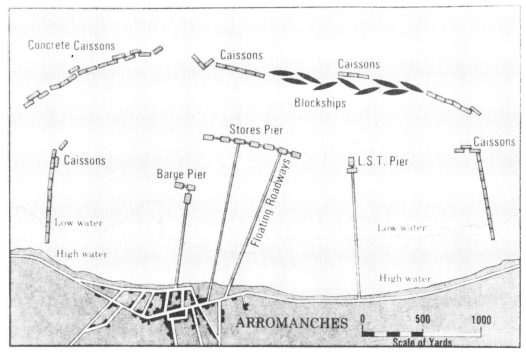

Concrete Caissons

Caissons

Caissons

Blockships

Stores Pier

Caissons

Caissons

L.S.T. Pier

Barge Pier

Floating Roadways

Low water

Low water

High water

High water

ARROMANCHES

0   500   1000

Scale of Yards

Mulberry harbour. More than two million tons of prefabricated steel and concrete were to be towed across the Channel to form the two artificial harbours.

lee of the specially-constructed steel breakwaters, known as "bombardons", to unload their back-up cargoes in relatively sheltered conditions.

Of course, these Mulberry harbours needed time to construct and assemble after being towed across the Channel – it would be four weeks before they were fully operational – but even on D-Day itself, after the little port of Arromanches had been captured, work on the Mulberry harbours began.

Not everything could be brought to the invading troops by ships unloading in the Mulberry harbours. Petrol to supply the vehicles was ingeniously piped from a pumping station in the south-east of England. A flexible aluminum alloy pipeline, laid on the bed of the Channel by cable-laying ships, ran to filling stations on the Normandy coast and by extension lines to stations further inland. It was known as PLUTO – Pipeline Under The Ocean.

The fishing villages and harbours in southern England would see a tremendous level of traffic involved in an operation such as OVERLORD. Sandy beaches could not withstand this, and so "hards" were constructed. These were slabs of concrete which could be lifted and moved by four men. These "hards" made serviceable loading areas over which vehicles could drive directly on to the shallow-draught landing craft at low water without any need for gangplanks, loading ramps or docks.

Final preparations

By 26 May the first invasion troops had been moved into "sealed" camps, from which they were not allowed out. Here they were briefed on their tasks and objectives. The final details were not given until the troops were at sea, at which time they were also issued with maps.

The invasion plan was explained to the General Officers of the Allied forces by Montgomery on 7 April 1944. On 15 May a final conference was held in London in the presence of King George VI, Winston Churchill and other high-ranking officers and officials. It was on this occasion that Montgomery outlined to them the intended plan for the Allied assault on Normandy.

Convoy of tanks heading for a south-coast port.

Why were the Germans taken by surprise?

As soon as the German High Command realized that an Allied invasion was inevitable, they concluded that it would come in the Pas de Calais. They never wavered from this belief, even when the invasion in Normandy was well under way. They were effectively blinkered from even considering that there might be other invasion areas. It was the area *they* would have chosen, as it was the shortest distance across the Channel and nearest to the industrial heartland of Germany. They were so convinced that the Pas de Calais was the only feasible invasion area that they concentrated their heaviest coastal defences there and stationed their toughest and most experienced troops and Panzer divisions within easy reach.

Building the Atlantic Wall beach defences. Much of the Wall was built by forced labour from various parts of Nazi-occupied Europe.

The Atlantic Wall, much of which was built by forced labour, ran from Denmark to Spain. It consisted of concrete blockhouses, gun emplacements, batteries, barbed wire entanglements, beach defences and mined areas – not all of it was an actual wall. It was stronger in some areas than in

others. Where natural defences such as cliffs, swamps and rocky shores prevailed, the Atlantic Wall was not as strongly built. However, Rommel had had the Atlantic Wall strengthened when he took over command in Normandy, despite the natural obstacles presented by the terrain. Even after this, however, the Normandy section of the Atlantic Wall was weaker than that in the Pas de Calais.

The German view of Normandy

As the German High Command, with the exception of Rommel, did not consider Normandy a serious target for an Allied invasion, the area was defended by fewer and, on the whole, less experienced troops than the Pas de Calais. It could be said that, in Normandy, the Germans relied too much on the natural defences of the coast and put too much faith in the Atlantic Wall's power to repel an invasion. Only von Rundstedt was not convinced of the merits of static defences and preferred to employ highly mobile troops to repel any invading force.

German experience of Allied invasions had been in North Africa, Sicily, and Italy – in none of these had the beaches been like those of Normandy. Previous Allied landings had been made in fine, calm weather at high tide – neither of which occurred early on 6 June 1944. The German High Command felt that in northern Europe the Allies would be sure to follow exactly their earlier invasion tactics. Consequently, they were confident that an Allied invasion of Normandy was unlikely, and would certainly not occur in early June, in bad weather and at low tide. They therefore took the opportunity offered by the forecasted bad weather for a little relaxation, regrouping, practice of manoeuvres and similar activities.

Problems with the German High Command

Reports transmitted by the notoriously unreliable German intelligence exaggerated the differences in opinion, background, attitude and experience of Allied leaders, and gave a picture of a divided command. While it was true that the commanders of SHAEF did not always see eye to eye and may not have always been the greatest of friends, they nonetheless pulled together when united against a common enemy. This was underestimated by the Germans, who thought that the Allied command would crack under the weight of difficulties and internal power struggles such as those experienced by the German High Command. But they reckoned without the diplomacy of Eisenhower, who somehow always managed to keep the team together.

German High Command, on the other hand, suffered from

continual differences of opinion between its leaders. These were exacerbated by Hitler playing off Rommel against von Rundstedt and at the same time wanting to control certain army units himself. Further divisions arose from the question of how an Allied invasion force should be counter-attacked. The result was often a lack of co-operation, cohesion and co-ordination just when these were most needed. Inflexibility and underestimation of the Allies, compounded with confusion and delay, cost the Germans dearly. Finally, at the crucial moment, too many key German generals were absent from their posts.

Allied deceptions pay off Above all, it was the clever and skilful deception practised by Allied intelligence which ensured that the Allies would have the element of surprise on their side. The programme of deception, known as Operation BODYGUARD, was ingenious, elaborate, meticulous and completely convincing. The Allies realized that it was impossible to hide the fact that they were building up an invasion force, so they made it seem as though all operations were concentrated in the south-east of England. They let it be known via double agents and carefully-prepared rumours that they would strike at the Pas de Calais during the last two weeks of July.

As part of the programme, dummy camps, roads and railways were set up in Kent, Sussex and East Anglia. Wireless messages were sent to fictitious army units which were supposedly camped in those areas. Dummy gliders were parked openly on airfields where they would be seen by German aerial reconnaissance. Dummy landing craft, ships, boats, tanks and lorries, often made from rubber and inflated like balloons, were assembled in and around the Kent ports and Essex. From the air these dummies looked like the real thing. A Combined Operations Group Headquarters was constructed at Dover, and it was from here that all Montgomery's wireless messages were transmitted. An entire American Army Group Headquarters, under the command of General George Patton, was "invented" and stationed in Kent. To add further credibility to the deception, General Patton and his conspicuous white dog were persuaded to be seen in the area. Such attention to detail was vital if Operation BODYGUARD was to be convincing.

Sporadic sorties by the Luftwaffe reported a massive build-up of troops in the south-east. Fewer trips were made over the longer and more dangerous stretch of the Channel coast to Portsmouth and Devon, where the real invasion force was

a

b

Operation Bodyguard – inflated tank, lorry and boats. These looked like the real thing to German reconnaissance aircraft.

gathered, so the report that went back to the German High Command confirmed their belief about the invasion site.

As late as 4 June, Admiral Kranke of the German Navy in the Channel expressed doubts as to whether the Allies had even assembled an invasion fleet. The bluff continued well into July, with the result that over a quarter of a million German troops were kept on alert for weeks in the Pas de Calais, waiting for the invasion that never came.

Until late July, Hitler himself continued to believe that the Normandy landings were merely a diversionary operation intended to lure troops away from the Pas de Calais. Too late, he realized that they were the real thing and that he had been successfully deceived.

D-Day was the best-kept secret of World War II.

Why did the Germans fail to hold Normandy?

Rommel had been right when he stated that if the Allied invasion was not defeated on the beaches, it would not be defeated at all. Nevertheless, he later maintained there would still be a chance of turning the tide after the Allies had landed. If the 12th SS Panzers could be brought into Caen to reinforce the weary 21st Panzers and the British could be driven back to the sea on the following day, 7 June, the Germans could regain their lost ground. With a flanking attack on the Canadians and a determined thrust at the precarious American hold on OMAHA Beach it might just be possible to re-establish the German position. But within 24 hours even that slim chance had been lost.

The race for Caen On the night of 6 June, British troops had dug themselves in near Lebisey, on the outskirts of Caen. On the following day, they renewed the attack and effectively held down the 21st Panzers. The 12th SS Panzers were divided – some were sent to prevent the Canadians capturing Carpiquet airfield, and some to push between the Canadians and the British. As the RAF had done such a good job in bombing petrol dumps, little fuel could be found for German tanks.

The British 50th Division held the Bayeux road. On OMAHA Beach the chaos had been sorted out and the American forces recovered sufficiently to move inland. The US airborne and seaborne troops were at last linking up and had fought off most German counter-attacks.

Because of the shortage of petrol for tanks, Panzer reserves were slow in coming to the scene. When they did arrive they were split up, so that at the critical moment the Germans were unable to launch a decisive counter-attack between Caen and Bayeux. Their forces were spread thinly along the 56-kilometre Allied bridgehead in an attempt to prevent a complete enemy breakthough. Despite being under constant attack from the air, the German line held.

The forces of the American General Bradley were able to take Carentan, which cut off the Cotentin Peninsula and Cherbourg. Although this joined the two American-held areas, there was stalemate until either side was able to bring reinforcements to the area. Eventually the Allies, despite the bad weather and length of time it took to cross the Channel, brought wave after wave of fresh troops into Normandy. The Germans were hindered by air strikes carried out by the RAF, and the sabotaging of railways by the Resistance movement prevented them from moving large bodies of troops into the area from elsewhere in France.

The Germans could not build up sufficiently quickly the mass of armed forces which Rommel had anticipated would attack from the south and separate the British and Americans. Allied follow-up troops threatened the entire length of the German line so that Rommel's armoured divisions had to be divided in order to give support where the threat was greatest. When the Panzers were eventually able to counter-attack, it was at only half strength.

The surprise The element of surprise was vital to the success of the
element Normandy invasion. The Germans never fully recovered from this, although they made some determined stands in the face of increasingly overwhelming odds. From the outset the Allies had superiority in the air – vital if they were to destroy supply bases and hinder German reinforcements from reaching the battle area.

The best German troops and crack Panzer divisions were stationed in the Pas de Calais. Allied action and confusion amongst the German High Command meant that these forces were slow to arrive in Normandy and, once there, were invariably divided. Consequently, Rommel's intended great counter-attack by massed troops, which was to smash the Allied line, never materialized. The Germans failed to contain the Allied "pockets" and "wedges" because of lack of weaponry and manpower. The German forces had been effectively divided into two fronts.

Hitler intervened personally, forbidding his forces to make an orderly retreat, although this would have given time to withdraw to new defences, rally, regroup and reorganize. As a result, the German army suffered staggering losses.

Lack of infantry was perhaps the main military reason for Germany's defeat in Normandy. In their misapprehensions concerning the invasion site, the Germans had stationed nineteen infantry divisions of the 15th Army east of the Seine. This reluctance to release troops from the area was one of the main reasons why the Germans lost the battle for Normandy.

Sabotage by the Resistance The Germans were unable to repair sufficiently quickly the damage done by the Allied interdiction campaign in the weeks and months preceding the invasion. Destroyed roads, bridges and railways hampered their ability to move troops to and around Normandy, to communicate effectively between their various headquarters, to maintain radar stations and airfields and to hold adequate supplies of equipment and petrol. The Luftwaffe had been rendered largely ineffective by Allied bombing of airfields. With roads constantly strafed by the RAF, bridges and railways blown up and telephone and telegraph wires cut, German communications were virtually non-existent. And without communications the German army was doomed.

Before arriving on the battlefield, many German reinforcing troops had undergone long journeys from other parts of Europe. They had made train journeys, undertaken long night marches when they could not be seen by Allied planes overhead, dived into ditches during the day to avoid strafing, hidden in woods and farms, and been soaked fording rivers and streams on foot. There was no time for them to rest and recover: exhausted, they were sent straight into battle.

A combination of German military and political mistakes and the sheer number of Allied troops which had been building up on the beaches ultimately resulted in Allied victory.

On 1 July the Germans made one last desperate bid to destroy the invaders, using four armoured divisions; but they were defeated by Scottish units. That evening von Rundstedt telephoned Field Marshal Keitel at Hitler's headquarters with the information that the battle for Normandy was lost. All chance of forcing the Allies back to the coast was gone.

"What shall we do?" asked Keitel.
"Make peace, you fools," replied von Rundstedt. "What else is there to do?"

Towards VE Day

To understand how von Rundstedt realized that the battle for Normandy was lost, it is necessary to go back to D-Day and the days immediately following. Within 48 hours of the first seaborne landings on 6 June, gaps in the Allied line were almost all closed to form a solid bridgehead. This then gradually pushed its way further and further inland until it was 30 kilometres in from the coast. Along this 130-kilometre line a fierce struggle between troops of both sides raged for several weeks. The Germans fought hard to maintain their line and from the middle of June there was virtual deadlock. A race to get reinforcements into the area followed.

The US 7th Corps under General Collins eventually cut off the Cotentin Peninsula, isolating the port of Cherbourg. There were enough troops to advance north and surround the port, and on 26 June the Germans there surrendered. By the end of the month the whole Cotentin Peninsula was safely in American hands and the next phase could begin. This involved American troops breaking through to the south, then swinging east to roll up the German line, beginning the move towards Paris.

Despite all this, the German High Command continued to believe that the Normandy landings were only a bluff. Panzer divisions were kept on the alert in the Pas de Calais for several weeks, waiting for the "real" invasion. This gave the Allies time to bring over reinforcements, although this advantage was lessened because bad storms and gales in the Channel virtually wrecked the Mulberry harbours and delayed the landing of follow-up troops, equipment and supplies. The American Mulberry harbour at Port-en-Bessin was virtually destroyed, and had to be abandoned.

Humans were not the only casualties. US troops take shelter behind dead cattle in the bocage country of Normandy.

Americans capture the Cotentin Peninsula

With Cherbourg secure in American hands, first the break-through in the west and south was accomplished. US troops then swept swiftly eastwards. Despite the *bocage* countryside, which favoured the Germans, the 7th Army was pushed further and further east until it was almost surrounded in the Falaise Pocket. The noose around the remnants of the 7th Army had been tightening for several weeks, with the action of the American 3rd Army from the south and the British 1st Corps from the north. The Germans fought desperately to keep open an escape route to the east, and fierce fighting continued until 19 August when the Falaise Gap was finally closed and many Germans were taken prisoner. Normandy was now virtually cut off from the rest of France, and fresh German troops could only be brought in by long, circuitous routes. Those Panzer Divisions which did manage to get through were divided to reinforce the existing German line.

German jokes about the Luftwaffe

The Luftwaffe continued to make sporadic off-shore night-time attacks on Allied shipping, and occasionally engaged RAF fighters raiding behind the German lines, but they were outnumbered and had little influence on events. Their lack of strike power was a joke even amongst the Germans, who said:

"When we see silver aircraft we know they're American. When we see coloured planes, they're British – when we don't see any at all, it's the Luftwaffe!"

The once-devastating combination of Luftwaffe and Panzers, which had swept all before it during the early years of the war, was no longer a force to be reckoned with.

A week after D-Day RAF bombers raided Boulogne and Le Havre, where German E-boats and other naval vessels were docked. They successfully eliminated the threat these posed to Allied shipping in the Channel by swamping, sinking, damaging or destroying the sixty or so ships moored in the two ports.

German prisoners of war pass dead horses near a Normandy farm. Note the attempt to camouflage the wagon with tree branches.

German doubts about Hitler

Ever since Rommel's forces had been driven out of North Africa in May 1943, level-headed people in Germany had begun to doubt the wisdom of Hitler's policies. Not everyone had agreed with his policies of over-running Europe and creating a "Thousand-Year Reich" (regime). Many, especially military men, began to see him as a fanatic. It was clear to them that the war, which had gone so well for them for the first three years, was now becoming a desperate struggle which Germany could not win. Some were so convinced that Hitler was leading Germany into disaster that they devised plots to assassinate him. As Hitler was a dictator they could not attempt to reason with him, talk to him, or try to persuade him to alter his ideas. To be seen to doubt his infallibility would, at the very least, incur his wrath and, more likely, result in being sent to a concentration camp or being executed.

The assassination attempt which came closest to succeeding occurred on 20 July 1944 (see *The July Plot* in this series). A young German army officer, Claus Graf Schenk von Stauffenberg, smuggled a bomb hidden in a briefcase into a meeting attended by Hitler. By sheer bad luck, someone moved the briefcase from its place near Hitler's chair and so, although the bomb went off, it failed to kill him.

The noose tightens

At this time, the middle of July, Allied troops were still pouring into Normandy, although many had returned to England in hospital ships. The follow-up troops no longer needed to fight their way across the beaches, and were able to bring more equipment, vehicles and ammunition into France. By the end of July the "build-up" period in Normandy was complete. The Allies, with almost one million British, American and Canadian troops, were ready for the push to the Seine, and then on across the Rhine. By the end of August all the Allied armies had crossed the Seine, driving German troops before them. They improvised all manner of boats, rafts and bridges in order to cross the river.

On the Eastern front, from Finland to the Black Sea, the Russians were staging a summer offensive designed to coincide with the Allied invasion in France. German forces were also retreating here. Germany was being squeezed in a vice-like grip from both south-east and west. Only two days before Allied troops began landing on the Normandy coast, British and American forces had entered Rome on their way north in the latest stage of a campaign begun in November 1942 when they had invaded North Africa.

It was possible to implement the Allied plan because of

For weeks after D-Day Allied troops and equipment continued to pour into Normandy. The barrage balloons were to prevent low-flying German aircraft strafing the Allied positions. Note that one has come adrift and rests on the deck of an LST (landing ship tank).

meticulous planning. Throughout the invasion, the Allies had kept the initiative and forced the Germans into fighting a defensive campaign.

The Germans fought with great tenacity and, arguably, if Hitler had interfered less with the decisions of the German High Command, the war might well have been a longer and even more bitterly contested struggle.

With the Russians driving German troops on the Eastern Front towards Germany and those in the west being driven from France, there were no remaining German forces to call on as reinforcements. The vice was tightening all the time. It became clear that Germany could not hold out much longer. But, even though many on both sides realized the end was in sight, German forces did not give up. It was the middle of August 1944 before the remnants of almost 18 German army formations were finally cleared from Normandy as Allied troops closed the Falaise Gap.

Could the war have been over by Christmas 1944?

A month later, in September, Allied paratroopers dropped into Nazi-occupied Holland at Arnhem, in a bid to end the war by Christmas 1944. They met stiff opposition, however, and suffered severe casualties.

Arnhem was followed by months of bitter fighting. Von Rundstedt's forces tried to push through the Ardennes in an attempt to divide the tiring British and American armies. Even though the 101st Airborne Division – veterans of the Cotentin Peninsula – were surrounded, they refused to surrender to the Germans. Finally, an 80-kilometre long smokescreen was used to give cover to the greatest single military airlift in history, when the Allies crossed the Rhine into the heart of industrial Germany.

Eleven months after D-Day itself, on 7 May 1945, all the well-timed and co-ordinated Allied campaigns in Europe finally bore fruit. This was Victory in Europe, VE Day, when Germany surrendered unconditionally to the Allies at Rheims.

Further reading

THE EVENTS

Hastings, Max, *Overlord: the day and the battle for Normandy 1944*, London, Michael Joseph, 1984
McElwee, William, *The Battle of D-Day*, London, Faber, 1965
Operation Overlord 1944-1984: the story of the Allied Invasion of Normandy. D-Day June 6 1944, Portsmouth and Sunderland Newspapers, 1984
Ryan, Cornelius, *The Longest Day*, London, Gollancz, 1960

THE INVESTIGATION

Belchem, David, *Victory in Normandy*, London, Chatto and Windus, 1981
Churchill, Winston S., *Triumph and Tragedy*, (Second World War), London, Cassell, 1954
Michie, Alan A., *Invasion of Europe: the Story Behind D-Day*, London, Allen and Unwin, 1964
Wilmot, Chester, *The Struggle for Europe*, London, Collins, 1952

Index